Theory Paper Grade 8   2007   A
Model Answers

1 *There are many ways of completing this question. The specimen completion below would receive full marks.* (15)
The source of the original adapted extract is: Corelli, Church Sonata, Op. 1 No. 2.

2 *There are many ways of completing this question. The specimen completion below would receive full marks.* (15)
 The source of the original adapted extract is: H. Lemoine, Piece in C major, Op. 37 No. 3.

3 *There are many ways of completing this question. Either of the specimen completions below would receive full marks.* (20)
*The given openings are printed in grey in order to distinguish them from the completion but candidates must include
the opening in their final answer.*

EITHER
TROMBONE

The source of the opening bars is: Haydn, String Quartet, Op. 20 No. 2, 2nd movt.

OR
OBOE

5

4 **(a)** slow and sad / slow and doleful / stately and sad / stately and doleful (2)

reinforced / sudden growth in volume (2)

(b) **A** Bar: 4 (2)

B Bar: 12 (2)

C Bar: 18 (2)

D Bar: 19 (2)

E Bar: 15 (2)

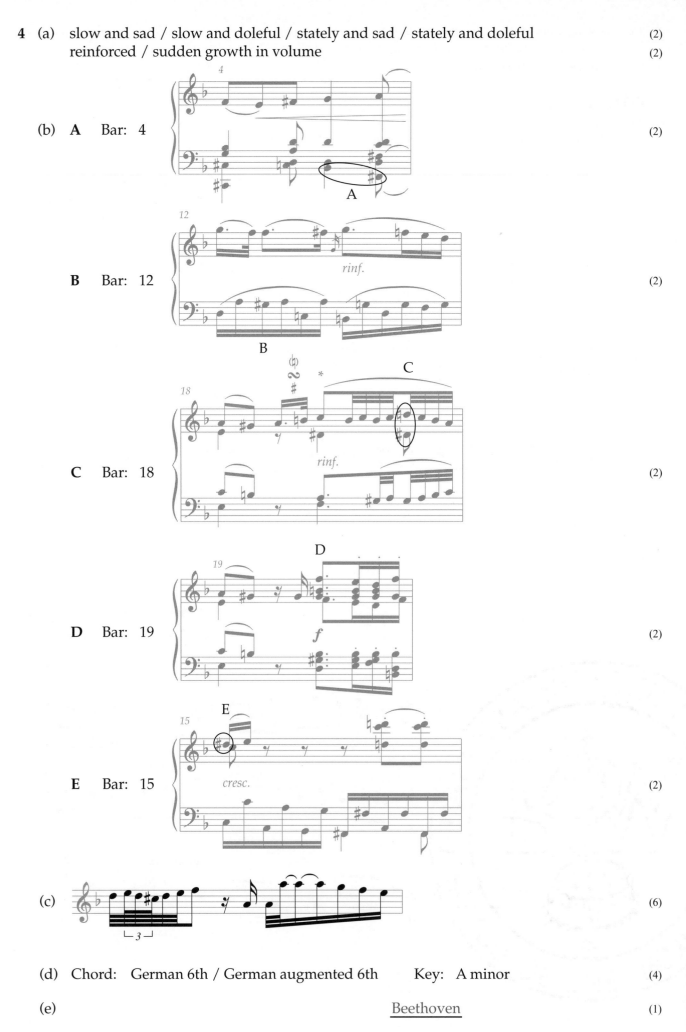

(c) (6)

(d) Chord: German 6th / German augmented 6th   Key: A minor (4)

(e) <u>Beethoven</u> (1)

5 (a) tenor trombones / trombones (2)
        timpani in E and B / kettledrums in E and B (3)

(b) (i)    (3)

     (ii) 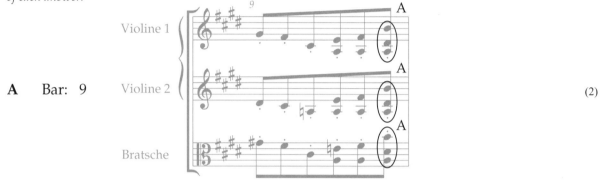 (5)

(c) *All possible answers for **A** are shown. For full marks candidates need to identify only one example of each answer.*

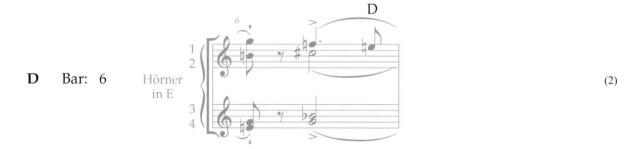

A Bar: 9   Violine 1 / Violine 2 / Bratsche (2)

B Bar: 6   Oboen 1 2 (2)

C Bar: 8   Klarinetten in A 1 2 (2)

D Bar: 6   Hörner in E 1 2 3 4 (2)

(d) (i)   false (2)
     (ii) false (2)

Theory Paper Grade 8   2007   B
Model Answers

1 *There are many ways of completing this question. The specimen completion below would receive full marks.* (15)
The source of the original adapted extract is: Corelli, Church Sonata, Op. 1 No. 9.

2 *There are many ways of completing this question. The specimen completion below would receive full marks.*
The source of the original adapted extract is: J. W. Hässler, No. 41 from 50 Pieces for Beginners.

3 *There are many ways of completing this question. Either of the specimen completions below would receive full marks.* (20)
   *The given openings are printed in grey in order to distinguish them from the completion but candidates must include
   the opening in their final answer.*

EITHER
OBOE

   The source of the opening bars is: F. Kirchner, Sonnenschein in Flur und Hain, Op. 270 No. 7.

OR
CELLO

4 (a) Bar 6: V ^{13} a major / V ^{13} a   Key: B♭ minor   (4)

        Bar 29: German 6th / German augmented 6th   Key: F minor   (4)

(b) 3–4; A♭ major; C minor; 4–6   (4)

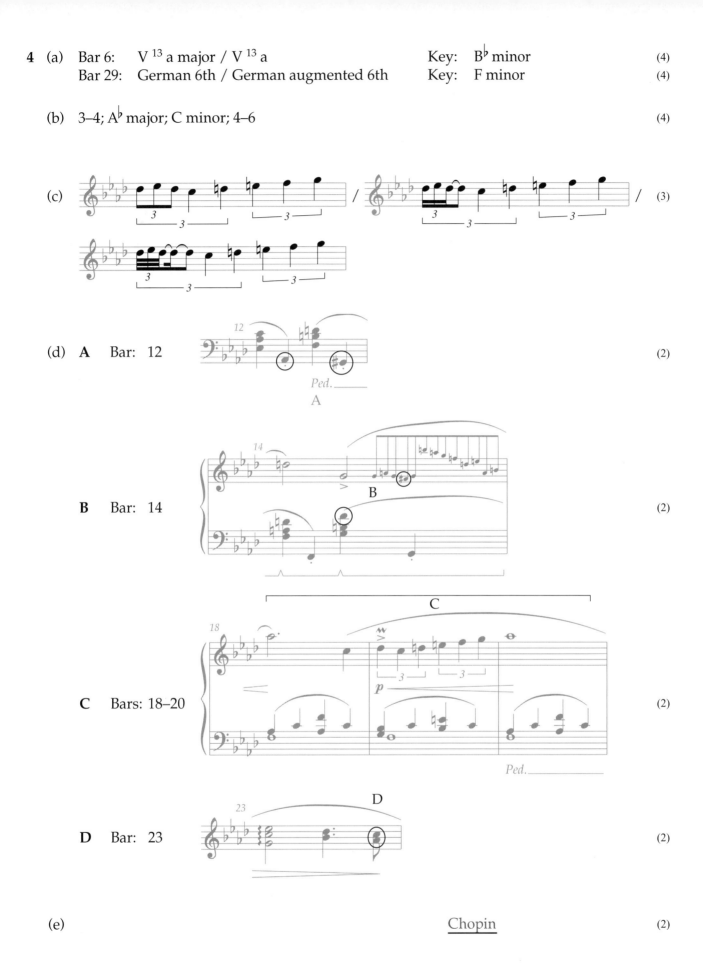

(c)   (3)

(d) **A**   Bar: 12   (2)

     B   Bar: 14   (2)

     C   Bars: 18–20   (2)

     D   Bar: 23   (2)

(e)   <u>Chopin</u>   (2)

5 **(a)** less animated / less lively (2)
enough / sufficiently / quite / fairly / very / extremely (1)
hurry / hurried / hurrying (2)

(b) **(i)** (4)

(ii) (2)

(c) starting quietly and gradually getting louder / starting quietly and getting louder (1)
up bow (1)
sliding the finger up the string from D to G (1)

(d) **(i)** alto flute / flute in G / bass flute (2)
(ii) 3 (2)
(iii) double bassoon; harp; double bass (3)

(e) (4)

Theory Paper Grade 8   2007   C
Model Answers

1 *There are many ways of completing this question. The specimen completion below would receive full marks.* (15)
The source of the original adapted extract is: Albinoni, Sonata da Camera.

2 *There are many ways of completing this question. The specimen completion below would receive full marks.* (15)
The source of the original adapted extract is: Fibich, Epilogue, from Moods, Impressions and Souvenirs.

3 *There are many ways of completing this question. Either of the specimen completions below would receive full marks.* (20)
The given openings are printed in grey in order to distinguish them from the completion but candidates must include the opening in their final answer.

EITHER
CELLO

>   *The source of the opening bars is: Schumann, Cello Concerto, Op. 129.*

OR
TRUMPET

4 (a) Bar 16:   German 6th / German augmented 6th   (3)
Bar 37:   Neapolitan 6th / ♭II b / ♭II b major   (3)

(b)   B; C; appoggiatura / leaning note   (3)

(c)   *All possible answers are shown on the extract reproduced on page 16. For full marks candidates need to identify only one example of each answer.*

A Bars: 17–21   (2)
B Bar: 2 / 6 / 14 / 26 / 34   (2)
C Bar(s):   13–14 / 21   (2)

(d) (i)   melodic line / same melody   (2)
    (ii) 1.   continuous quavers in left-hand part   (2)
          2.   falling chromatic bass line / more frequent changes of harmony   (2)

(e)   (4)

16

5 (a) slow (2)

drum roll / rapid reiteration of the same note (2)

tender / delicate / soft (2)

(b) (i)
(3)

(ii)
(5)

(c) (i) first oboe; 8–9; 12–13; 14–15 (4)

(ii) diminished 7th (2)

(d) Chord: Italian 6th / Italian augmented 6th (3)

(e) <u>Wagner</u> (1)

German terms exclude Puccini and Elgar and are unlikely for Brahms / (1)
harmonic language

Theory Paper Grade 8   2007   S
Model Answers

1 *There are many ways of completing this question. The specimen completion below would receive full marks.*   (15)
  The source of the original adapted extract is: Corelli, Church Sonata, Op. 3 No. 12.

2 *There are many ways of completing this question. The specimen completion below would receive full marks.* (15)
The source of the original extract is: Grechaninov, Lullaby, from Children's Book Op. 98.

3 *There are many ways of completing this question. Either of the specimen completions below would receive full marks.* (20)
The given openings are printed in grey in order to distinguish them from the completion but candidates must include the opening in their final answer.

EITHER
OBOE

The source of the opening bars is: Brahms, Sextet, Op. 36 No. 2.

OR
VIOLIN

4 (a)   Bar 23:   ♭II^{7}d / ♭II^{7}d major   (3)

         Bar 30:   V$^{♭9}$a / V$^{♭9}$a major   Key: C minor   (4)

   (b)   *All possible answers are shown on the extract reproduced below.*

       A   Bars: 26–29   (2)

       B   Bar(s):   22–23   (2)

       C   Bar: 26   (2)

       D   Bar: 27   (2)

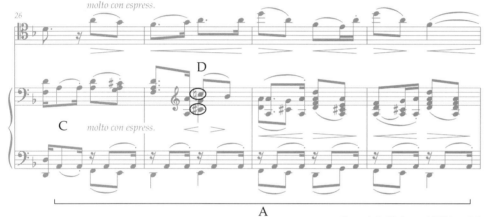

   (c)   (i)   19–26;   (1)

       One mark will be awarded (up to a maximum of two marks) for each correct reference to:

       octave higher / length of final note / cello moves into the tenor clef /   (2)
         B♮ in bar 24;

       harmony / rhythm final quaver bar 21 / change in bass line bars 23–26   (1)

       (ii)   much with expression / very expressive / very with expression   (2)

   (d)    (4)

5 (a) a joke / a playful movement / title of a fast movement / title of a playful movement (2)
very lively / much lively (2)
drum roll / rapid reiteration of the same note (2)

(b) **A**   Bar: 13    (2)

Both possible answers are shown on the extract reproduced below. For full marks candidates need to identify only one example of each answer.

B   Bar: 5  (2)

(c)

Clarinets (4)

Trumpets (3)

(d) (i) 7; 24 (2)
(ii) $\flat$· (2)
(iii) 13 / 13–14 (2)
(iv) 2 / 4 (2)

Theory of Music Exams Model Answers are a useful resource for pupils and teachers preparing for ABRSM theory exams. They are available for the 2007 Theory of Music Exams Past Papers, Grades 1 to 8.

Music theory publications from ABRSM Publishing include:

Theory of Music Exams Past Papers
Grades 1 to 8 (separately)

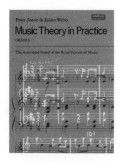

Music Theory in Practice
Grades 1 to 5 (separately)
by Eric Taylor

Grades 6 to 8 (separately)
by Peter Aston & Julian Webb

Theory Workbook
Grades 6 to 8 (separately)
by Anthony Crossland

The AB Guide to Music Theory
Parts I and II
by Eric Taylor

PUBLISHING

The Associated Board of
the Royal Schools of Music
(Publishing) Limited

24 Portland Place
London W1B 1LU
United Kingdom

www.abrsmpublishing.com

ISBN 978-1-86096-889-1

9 781860 968891